Arctic, apple, aurora, Anik
Bonhomme, Bluenose, beaver, bannock

Canadarm, Cavendish, chinook, caribou
Dory, dinosaur, dulse, Dan McGrew

Evangeline, evergreen, eh?, Expo
Fleur-de-lis, fiddlehead, Fox, Fogo

Gould, Gretzky, Greene, grizzly bear
Habitant, Horseshoe, humpback, hare

Imax, insulin, Iqaluit, ice blind
Jay, Jasper, Juno, jack pine

Klondike, komatik, kittiwake, kayak
Loon, lacrosse, Lillooet, lumberjack

Maple, moose, McClung, Mountie
Neepawa, narwhal, nickel, Napanee

Ogopogo, Ottawa, oil, osprey
Peterson, potlatch, poutine, Percé

Quahog, quarter horse, quints, Qu'Appelle
Rockies, railway, rodeo, Riel

Shediac, sockeye, spud, St-Hubert
Tuktoyaktuk, toque, totem, tourtière

Ungava, umiak, uranium, ulu
Voyageur, Villeneuve, Viking, Van Doo

Wheat, walleye, Wawa, waxwing
Xenon, xylograph, X-country, X-ing

Yarmouth, Yoho, York, Yellowhead
Zamboni, zipper, zinc, zed

A Canadian ABeCedarium

Eh?
to Zed

Kevin Major

Illustrated by Alan Daniel

Red Deer Press

Arctic, apple, aurora, Anik

Bonhomme, Bluenose, beaver, bannock

Canadarm, Cavendish, chinook, caribou

Dory, dinosaur, dulse, Dan McGrew

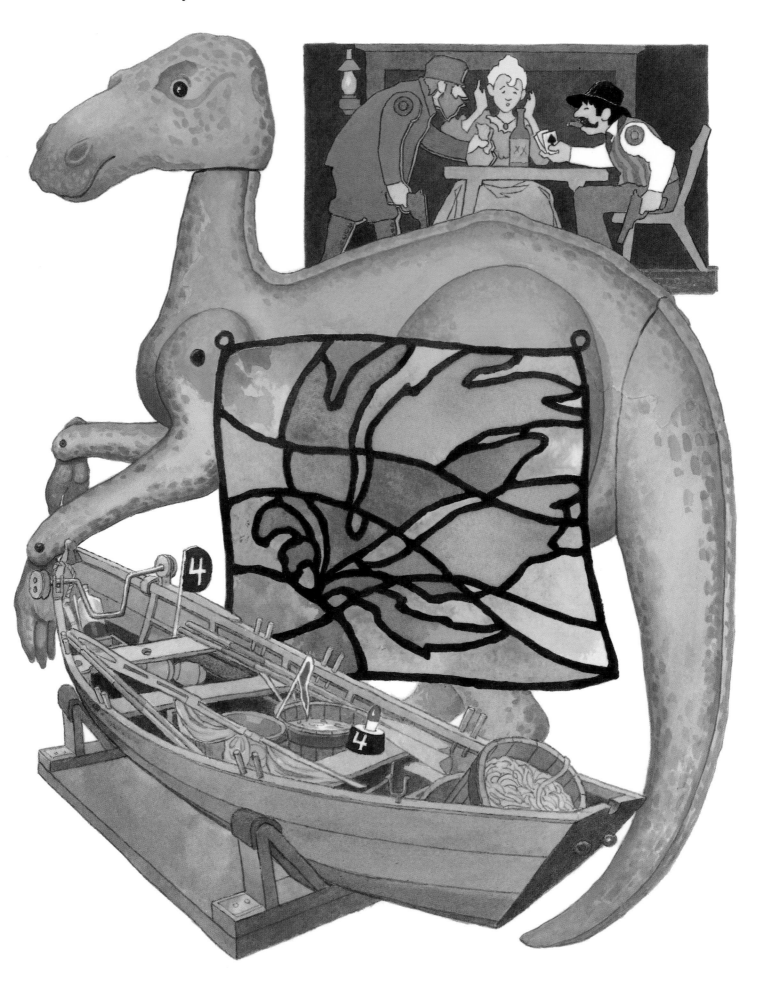

Evangeline, evergreen, eh?, Expo

Fleur-de-lis, fiddlehead, Fox, Fogo

FOGO, FOGO IS.

Gould, Gretzky, Greene, grizzly bear

Habitant, Horseshoe, humpback, hare

Imax, insulin, Iqaluit, ice blind

Jay, Jasper, Juno, jack pine

Klondike, komatik, kittiwake, kayak

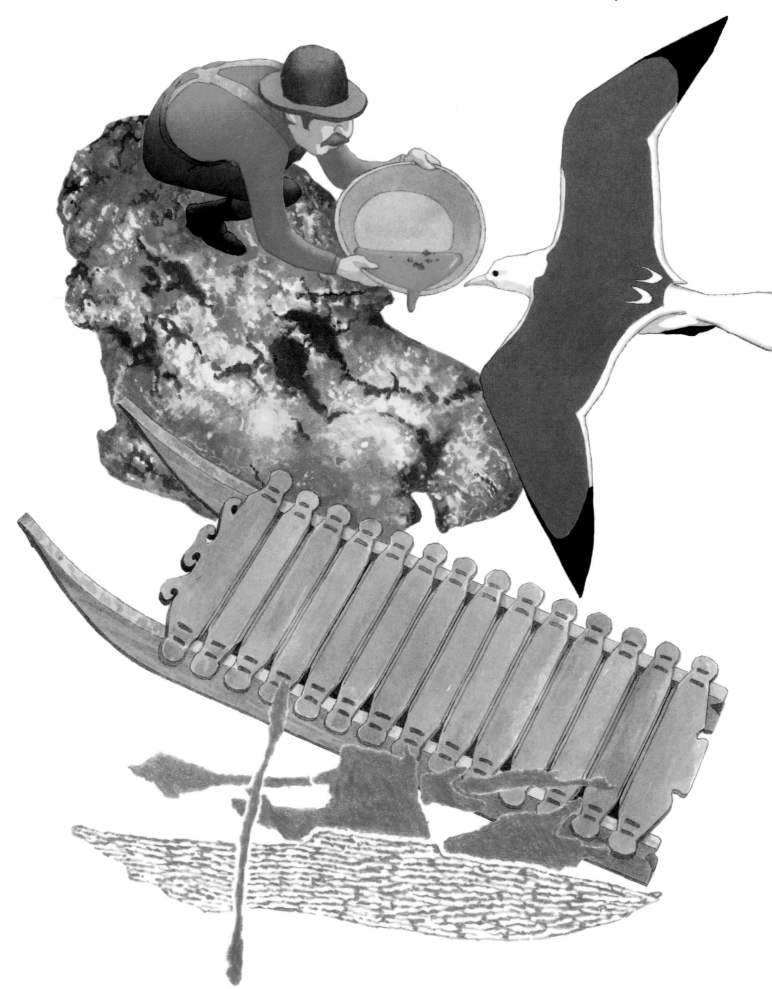

Loon, lacrosse, Lillooet, lumberjack

Maple, moose, McClung, Mountie

Neepawa, narwhal, nickel, Napanee

Ogopogo, Ottawa, oil, osprey

Peterson, potlatch, poutine, Percé

Quahog, quarter horse, quints, Qu'Appelle

A.P.   Katepwa Lake

Qu'Appelle Valley

Rockies, railway, rodeo, Riel

Shediac, sockeye, spud, St-Hubert

Tuktoyaktuk, toque, totem, tourtière

Ungava, umiak, uranium, ulu

Voyageur, Villeneuve, Viking, Van Doo

Wheat, walleye, Wawa, waxwing

Xenon, xylograph, X-country, X-ing

Yarmouth, Yoho, York, Yellowhead

My Dad's Boat by Marie, Yarmouth, N.S.

DIANE MARIE

LEAUCHOIL HOODOOS, YOHO NATIONAL PARK, B.C.

Zamboni, zipper, zinc, zed

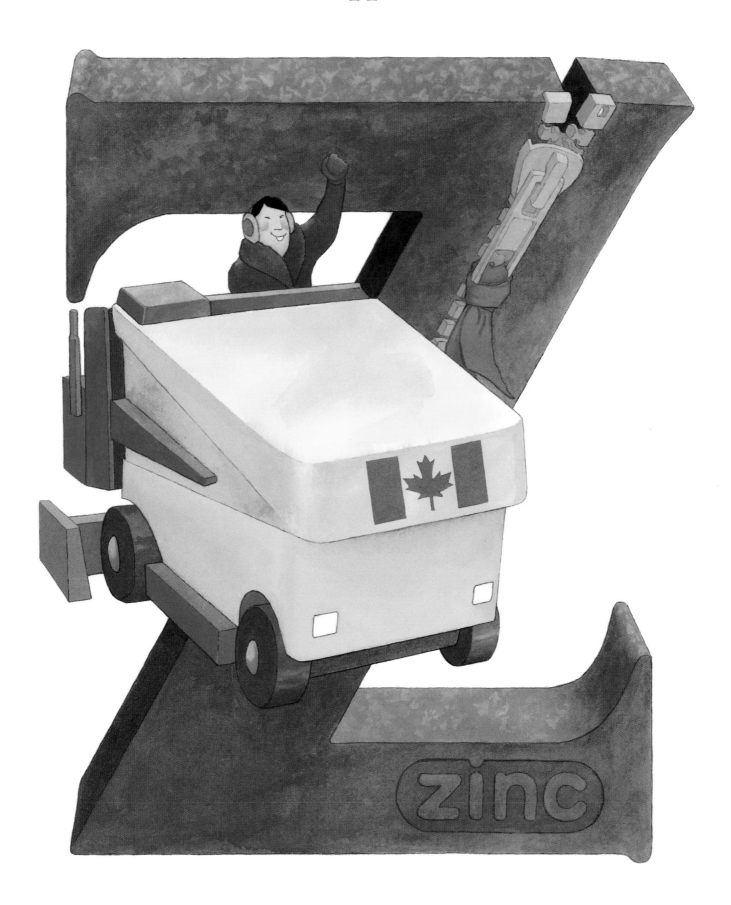

THE CHOICE OF WORDS, THE CHOICE OF IMAGES

Kevin Major's caravan of words cheers our history and celebrates our heroes. It couples the well known with the obscure, the curious with the symbols of our nation. For every province and territory there is a place name, for many junctions of our country something to be discovered. Here are some morsels of information the author came up with for the 104 words.

In most of the **ARCTIC** there is at least one day each winter when the sun never rises and one day each summer when it never sets. Neither the arctic fox, the arctic char, nor the arctic poppy seems to mind. • Long before the age of computers, the **APPLE** became Canada's favoured fruit. All the McIntosh apples ever eaten are descended from the tree discovered by John McIntosh while he was clearing his land at Dundela, Ontario, in 1811. • In Inuit mythology the Northern Lights, **AURORA** Borealis, were torches to guide new arrivals into heaven, while in medieval Europe they were the traces of dead soldiers still in battle. • **ANIK** was the world's first satellite with a shaped antenna beam designed to cover the entire territory of one country. It added a new dimension to Canada's motto, *A Mari usque ad Mare* (From Sea to Sea), in this case, from the Atlantic to the Pacific to the Arctic.

BONHOMME Carnaval is the snowman mascot of Québec City's midwinter *fête*. From his home in an ice castle, he warms the hearts of thousands with his *joie de vivre*. • A string of victories in the International Fisherman's Cup in the 1920s and '30s makes the **BLUENOSE** Canada's most famous ship. Since 1937 a picture of this Lunenburg-built schooner can be had for a dime. • Our flat-tailed friend the **BEAVER** is an official emblem of Canada and appeared on our first postage stamp. Not bad for a rodent. • A true Canuck prefers his **BANNOCK** made over an open fire and with a frypan that's tilted so the bread bakes from the top. Ingredients: flour, water, salt, baking powder, and, of course, a little back bacon grease. The Shuttle Remote Manipulator System, the **CANADARM**, retrieves satellites and lends a hand to space walkers. It made Roberta Bondar, Julie Payette, and our other astronauts feel even more at home. • Lucy Maud Montgomery's *Anne of Green Gables* was rejected five times before it found a publisher. Today her childhood home in **CAVENDISH**, Prince Edward Island, draws 350,000 visitors a year. • Albertans know **CHINOOK** as a warm, dry wind that gives a day of summer in the middle of February. British Columbians, who already have the warmest winter weather in Canada, just think of it as another salmon ready for the barbecue. • **CARIBOU**, like most Canadians, have learned to shovel snow. We uncover cars; caribou use their heads and uncover food. The **DORY** was the workhorse of the greatest cod fishery of the world, off Newfoundland. Dories were rowed or sailed to the inshore fishing grounds or stacked one atop another on the decks of schooners heading for the Grand Banks. • The T-rex– like *Albertosaurus* liked nothing better than chasing down prime rib with its mouthful of razor teeth. Amid the **DINOSAUR**-eat-dinosaur world of Alberta, the duck-billed *Edmontosaurus* preferred to dine quietly on a salad of twigs, seeds, and conifer shoots. • Grand Manan Island in the Bay of Fundy lays claim to the best **DULSE** anywhere. The seaweed is picked at low tide and sun-dried, munched as is or maybe pan-fried. • Is there a more famous character in Canadian verse than Robert Service's Dangerous **DAN McGREW**? Not unless it's Sam McGee or "the lady that's known as Lou." Longfellow's poem *EVANGELINE* tells of exiled Acadians from Nova Scotia who find a home in Louisiana in the mid-1700s. It is Canadian history that was for centuries on the lips of American school children. • On our Pacific coast can be found the largest tree in Canada, a 400-year-old sitka spruce. This **EVERGREEN** stands 95 metres tall and comes with its own name — the Carmanah Giant. • Canada's 30 million people are scattered over the world's second-largest country. And ours is a multilingual people, **EH?**, so we need some common expressions to unite us. • Montreal's **EXPO** in 1967 and Vancouver's in 1986 are remembered for their innovative architecture. Also built on innovation were Les Expos, the first major league baseball team outside the United States. The flag of Québec bears the ancient French symbol of the stylized lily. On St-Jean-Baptiste Day, June 24, the streets of Québec are abloom with the **FLEUR-DE-LIS**. • Coiled on a dinner plate, the **FIDDLEHEAD** is a tasty spring vegetable. Uncoiled in nature, it is an ostrich fern. • In 1980, having lost a leg to cancer, Terry **FOX** began his run across Canada. Each September the courage of "Canada's Greatest Hero" inspires thousands at home and around the world to continue his "Marathon of Hope." • The Flat Earth Society claims Brimstone Head, on **FOGO** Island, Newfoundland, as one of the four corners of the earth. Skeptics should also know that others have been pinpointed in Siberia, Papua New Guinea, and Easter Island. At age 12 Glenn **GOULD** played the piano in a Kiwanis Music Festival. He took first place and ten dollars, not the last time he would show his winning ways with a Bach prelude and fugue. • At age 11 Wayne **GRETZKY** finished up his Brantford minor hockey season with 378 goals. It was a strong hint that one day he would rewrite the National Hockey League record book. • It was not until age 14 that Nancy **GREENE** started to take ski racing seriously. Yet within 10 years our "Female Athlete of the Century" retired with a giant slalom and two World Cup titles, plus Olympic gold. • The **GRIZZLY BEAR** gets its name from patches of grizzled fur that make it look older than it really is. Yet one blow from even an adolescent forearm can kill any animal of equal size. In old Québec a **HABITANT** was a permanent settler who lived on the land. In the Québec of recent times a Hab played hockey in Montréal and won a string of Stanley Cups. • The **HORSESHOE** Falls of the mighty Niagara is our most visited natural wonder. On

March 30, 1848, visitors saw it run dry, then gush 30 hours later when the ice jam broke. • A meal for a **HUMPBACK** consists of 1,000 kilograms of ocean tidbits. Fortunately for krill and plankton, the whale sticks to two meals a day. • What woodsmen call a rabbit is actually a snowshoe **HARE**. Its paws inspired our First Nations people to devise a way of walking through deep snow. • With the invention of **IMAX** ("eye" to the max), Canadians have transformed the motion picture experience. The first permanent Imax theatre was in Ontario Place; the first permanent feature was *North of Superior*. • **INSULIN** was discovered in 1922 through experiments led by Frederick Banting and Charles Best at the University of Toronto. After trials on a diabetic dog, it was 14-year-old Leonard Thompson who became the first human to receive an injection. • **IQALUIT** is the capital of Nunavut, which makes up our central and eastern Arctic. It stands at the southern end of Baffin Island, the largest island in Canada and the fifth largest in the world. • An **ICE BLIND** is made of ice blocks that conceal an ice hunter, who wears ice goggles to prevent ice blindness. Canadian dictionaries list dozens of words that relate to ice, and after the Ice Storm of 1998 there are likely to be even more.

In the woods the blue **JAY** always makes himself heard, especially in the autumn. Not unlike the baseball variety, who also has lots to shout about, like capturing the World Series two Octobers in a row. • Centuries ago **JASPER**, Alberta, was a stopping point for a few furriers with the stamina to venture through the Rocky Mountains. Today it's a stopping point for thousands of tourists with a yen for spectacular scenery. • We like to give our **JUNO** Awards to musical giants before the Grammy Awards discover them. Just ask Céline, Sarah, Shania, Alanis, or k.d. • Before Tom Thomson and the Group of Seven showed up on the shores of Georgian Bay, the **JACK PINE** was just a tree. Now it's an icon of Canadian art. In 1897 a hundred thousand dreamers headed for the Yukon. Overnight, the **KLONDIKE** Gold Rush turned Dawson into the biggest place west of Winnipeg and the wildest town in Canada. • A **KOMATIK** is an Inuit sled traditionally pulled by a team of dogs. Now the sleds are as likely to be trailing behind snowmobiles as they are huskies. • The **KITTIWAKE** gets its name from its distinctive cry. That and its black-tipped wings single it out from the colonies of gulls, puffins, murres, and gannets along our Atlantic coast. • The recreational **KAYAK** of the ecotourist had its origin in the far North. By necessity the first were made of stretched seal and caribou hides rather than rotationally moulded polyethylene. The **LOON** was the image of choice when our dollar coin replaced our dollar bill. And in our Canadian wilderness, far from banks and stores, the loon, with its haunting call, is worth its weight in gold. • **LACROSSE**, the oldest organized sport on the continent, was invented by native tribes to settle disputes and train warriors. There were hundreds of players to a side, the playing ground was the size of four football fields, and matches lasted two or three days. • During the 1860s **LILLOOET**, British Columbia, was Mile 0 on the Cariboo Road, and led to the gold fields of the Cariboo and Fraser rivers. A century later it was home to Canada's most renowned newspaper woman, Ma Murray, who promised "a chuckle every week and a belly laugh once a month or your money back." • Next to the Mountie, the **LUMBERJACK** is seen by the world as the most Canadian of occupations. But whereas the Mountie gets to cry, "We always get our man!" the lumberjack can only yell, "Tim—berrr!" It adorns our flag, colours our forests, and brings syrup to our tables. We sing the praises of the **MAPLE** leaf forever. • The **MOOSE** has a humped back, legs like stilts, a bulbous snout with a protruding upper lip, and a hairy pouch of skin dangling from its throat. Not our best-looking beast, but a popular one, found in the woods of almost every province and territory, and even on some city streets. • Under the leadership of Nellie **McCLUNG**, the suffragists of the prairie provinces were the first in Canada to win the vote for women. In McClung's words, "Never retreat, never explain, never apologize — get the thing done and let them howl." • A scarlet-coated **MOUNTIE** on a trusty horse makes the RCMP Musical Ride a patriotic wonder to behold. Not even Disney can brandish such split-second perfection. **NEEPAWA**, Manitoba, is the birthplace of writer Margaret Laurence. Her *Stone Angel* and *Olden Days Coat* are among the many works that have given our literature its world-class reputation. • The **NARWHAL** has a spiralling upper tooth that can reach a length of three metres. Scientific evidence shows that sometimes the adult males would rather joust than eat. • Sudbury's monumental Big **NICKEL** measures nine metres tall and in 1964 cost $35,000 to make. That's 700,000 nickels and worth every penny. • During the American Revolution many who remained true to Britain headed to Canada. One of the many places settled by these United Empire Loyalists is **NAPANEE**, Ontario, whose annual Walleye Fishing Derby still draws people from the other side of the border. Lake Okanagan's 20-foot **OGOPOGO** predates the Loch Ness Monster by several years. And not only does it have fuzzy pictures to prove its existence, but the sworn testimony of a ship's captain, a priest, and a policeman. • **OTTAWA** is home to the largest skating rink in the world — an eight-kilometre stretch of the Rideau Canal. Some of the many politicians who inhabit our country's capital city use this slippery surface to keep in shape. • The first commercial petroleum well in North America was drilled in Ontario in 1858. And thanks to Canadian ingenuity, **OIL** of a different sort — the nutritionally superior canola — has surged onto world markets. • The **OSPREY** has sharp, curved claws, nostrils that close, a reversible outer toe, and spikes on the sole of each foot. All good reasons for also calling it the fish hawk. In addition to receiving countless international music awards, jazz legend Oscar **PETERSON** is a Companion of the Order of Canada and holds a dozen honorary degrees. In Canada we like to celebrate the best. • Among the native people of the Northwest a **POTLATCH** is a great ceremonial event marked by powerful speeches. As in any culture, when the speeches are over the fun part begins — gift giving, spirit dancing, and feasting that lasts several days. • Probably not on any ceremonial menu is **POUTINE**. This combo of French fries, cheese curds, and gravy is a taste sensation inspired by the Québec of the 1950s. • For centuries **PERCÉ** on the Gaspé Peninsula has attracted visitors to the sight of its famed offshore monolith. It stands as the most photographed rock in Canada. Some people know it as the "hard-shelled clam" or the "steamer clam" or the "cherrystone clam," and because its shell was used as a form of money, scientists called it *mercenaria mercenaria*. But to most of us it's the **QUAHOG**. • We'll admit the **QUARTER HORSE** was bred south of the border when English horses were crossed with Spanish ones. But nowhere do they better display their talents than on the cattle ranches north of the 49th parallel. • The birth of the Dionne **QUINTS** — Annette, Cécile, Emilie, Marie, and Yvonne — in rural Ontario in 1934 was seen as a miracle in the midst of the Depression. But the most enduring message of their lives has been about the rights of children. • **QU'APPELLE** in Saskatchewan has the most romantic derivation of any place name in Canada: a Cree warrior paddling his canoe heard someone call his name, but when he answered, "Qu'appelle?" there was no reply. It had been the voice of his beloved, ill and calling to him with her last breath, as she still does upon the prairie winds. Alberta and British Columbia share the Canadian **ROCKIES**. The history of this spectacular mountain range is one of ruggedness, as the name Kicking Horse Pass would seem to indicate. • It was the promise in 1871 of a **RAILWAY** that lured British Columbia into becoming a province. Fourteen years later the Last Spike was driven home and captured in the most famous photograph in Canadian history. • The Calgary Stampede bills itself as the "Greatest Outdoor Show on Earth." Now that's a **RODEO**. • Métis leader Louis **RIEL** is a founding father of Manitoba. His hanging in 1885 was a tragic moment in the history of all Canadians. **SHEDIAC**, New Brunswick, is the "Lobster Capital of the World." The fact that it's been holding a Lobster Festival each summer for over half a century just proves it. • The **SOCKEYE**, like other species of Pacific salmon — the pink, the chum, the coho, and the chinook — has evolved a life cycle that continues to astound scientists. It hatches in an inland stream, swims to the open ocean, lives there for years, then navigates 1,000 kilometres or more back to the very place it was born. • Each year farmers on Prince Edward Island produce almost 10 tonnes of potatoes per resident. Rather a good reason for people to call it **SPUD** Island and for Islanders to open a Potato Museum. • **ST-HUBERT** is to barbecued chicken what Tim Horton's is to doughnuts. Both are prime places to talk about the weather. Northerners call it "Tuk." But the western Arctic community's full name is **TUKTOYAKTUK**, meaning "resembles a caribou," all because the land on which it stands is shaped like an antler. • Can a **TOQUE** be a toque without a tassel? Only as long as it keeps your head and ears from freezing. • **TOTEM** poles of the Pacific Northwest tell intriguing stories of native culture. The red cedar ages, but the stories never grow old. • In frontier times the passenger pigeon was a favourite ingredient in a **TOURTIÈRE**. Today it's the minced pork variety of the pie that emerges from ovens all over French Canada in the early hours of Christmas morning. The U-shaped **UNGAVA** Bay of the eastern Arctic turns into the N-shaped Ungava Peninsula, which holds a nearly perfectly O-shaped meteor crater. The crater is 3.4 kilometres wide and forms the deepest lake in Québec. • The **UMIAK** is the large, open boat of the Inuit. Men paddled the craft during whaling expeditions; women took charge when transporting their families. • **URANIUM**, the heaviest element occuring in nature, has a density 19 times greater than water. Strong Canadians recover more of it than any other people in the world. • An ordinary **ULU** is a knife used by northern native women for scraping and cutting. A gold ulu is an award given to first-place winners at the Arctic Winter Games. Long before the Voyager of space, there was the **VOYAGEUR** of New France. Around the campfire at night, he told the legend of *la chasse-galerie*, a canoe that could fly. • Gilles **VILLENEUVE** and his son Jacques are Canada's gift to the world of auto racing. In 1978 Gilles claimed the first of his six Formula One wins; in 1997 Jacques captured the Formula One World Championship. • Leif Ericsson's **VIKING** expedition landed at L'Anse aux Meadows, Newfoundland, about the year 1000 A.D. With the encounter between his people and the natives of Vinland, the human race had circled the globe. • **VAN DOO** is a corruption of *vingt-deux*, the name the English have given the famed Royal 22e Régiment. In both languages Canada's veterans and peacekeepers deserve a loud bravo! **WHEAT** is Canada's most important crop, with over 30 million tonnes grown each year, the majority of it in Saskatchewan. Someone somewhere is making a lot of bread. • Canada has room for plenty of **WALLEYE** and their anglers. Nearly two million lakes to be exact. • **WAWA** means "wild goose" in the Ojibwa language. Every year thousands of people stop by this Ontario town to take a gander at its nine-metre-high statue of a Canada goose. • Other birdwatching Canadians keep their eyes peeled for the **WAXWING** and the sealing-wax–like touch of red on its wing feathers. Only the sharpest eyes can tell the difference between the two species found in Canada — the cedar and the Bohemian. **XENON** is colourless, odourless, tasteless, and inert. Not exactly Canadian, or is it? This gas illuminates the lighthouses dotting our coasts — the beacons that for many immigrants were the first sign of their new home. • As the printmakers of the 1930s will attest, the **XYLOGRAPH** was a natural artistic expression for Canadians. This engraving technique uses an end-grain block from the maple tree. • "Jackrabbit" Johannsen, the father of

THE CHOICE OF WORDS, THE CHOICE OF IMAGES

X-COUNTRY skiing in Canada, declared it to be the healthiest of our winter sports. Who's to argue with someone who lived to be 111? • The railway X-ING has long been a fixture on the Canadian landscape. Around the world, trains cross time zones as well as roads, thanks to the creation of standard time by our great railway builder, Sandford Fleming.

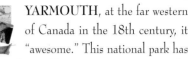

YARMOUTH, at the far western shores of Nova Scotia, is a seaport with strong ties to New England. Like other parts of Canada in the 18th century, it was a port of call for slaves escaping America. • In the Cree language YOHO means "awesome." This national park has an awesome collection of mountains, lakes, and waterfalls, and one of the most yoho fossil sites in the world. • YORK Factory was the premier outpost of the Hudson's Bay Company. The term *York boat* is derived from it, but not the city of York, the place which now calls itself Toronto. • YELLOWHEAD Pass through the Rockies was named after a blond Iroquois trapper and guide, Tête Jaune. It was a distinct improvement over its first name — Leather Pass — and especially over its second — Cowdung Pass. A Canadian, Bombardier, invented the snowmobile, and it seems only logical that a Canadian should also have invented the ZAMBONI. But, alas, the only claim Canadians can make is that they see this California invention in more hockey arenas at six in the morning than any other people on earth. • But Pablum we did invent, along with the paint roller, Muskol, green garbage bags, Trivial Pursuit, and the ZIPPER. We first tried to market the zipper by another name, but had trouble saying, "Your Talon Slide Fastener is down." • Canada's rock legend Neil Young titled one of his many classic albums *Rust Never Sleeps*. Could he have been inspired by the fact that his homeland is the world's second largest producer of ZINC, the element that gives steel a great resistance to rust? Just maybe. • And what is the last letter of the Canadian alphabet? ZED. It rhymes with *red*, like the maple leaf on our flag. We wear our words proudly!

Alan Daniel's response to these 26 quartets of words reflects the cultural artefacts that have emerged throughout our history. The tableaus he has created are filled with both folk and fine art, the sacred as well as the commercial. They are objects to display in museums and toys to fill a child's idle hours. Several of them call for special mention.

From the distant past grew the art of our First Nations people. The KAYAK and its hunter are depicted by a drawing on rock, a petroglyph. The HUMPBACK is a soapstone carving, the HARE is whalebone inlaid with antler. The Raven hat would have been worn by a Tlingit chief at a POTLATCH, the number of rings on the hat indicating the number of such feasts he had hosted. From the Six Nations comes a cornhusk doll holding a LACROSSE racket, from the Mi'kmaq a MOOSE-caller of quillwork on birchbark. Several native peoples turned the shell of the QUAHOG into polished beads for wampum belts.

The arrival of a VIKING expedition — here in the style of an 11th century Bayeux tapestry — marked the infusion of the landscape with a new array of artefacts. Might these people have been the ones to raise the ancient stone structure that stands beside the Payne River in UNGAVA. Is it a cross or hammer of Thor? No one knows for sure.

A succession of French and English settlers landed on our shores, bringing their handiwork with them and changing it to suit their new surroundings. Sheet iron FLEUR-DE-LIS would have been seen atop the 18th century French fortress at Louisbourg. DULSE takes shape in stained glass, MAPLE sugar leaves in a carved wooden mould. An image of Terry FOX is lovingly formed by intricate paper cutting. The X-COUNTRY skier emerges from a cutting of a polished woodblock.

Even the most everyday of items, a painted iron trivet — becomes a work of art when it takes on the form of a FIDDLEHEAD. The tin fish CHINOOK, the CARIBOU weathervane, and the whirligig Mountie, EH?, with arms that reel in the wind, all brought the world of imagination to the home.

When we ventured out as tourists in our own country, to places such as YOHO, the postcards we sent home were black and white photographs tinted by artistic hands. And when native peoples saw what new materials others had brought, they adapted them to their own uses. An oil barrel in TUKTOYAKTUK is restructured into a trapper's stove.

Just as we pass along our Canadian words to our children, we pass along our crafts in the objects of their play. A miniature KOMATIK from Labrador is a companion for an Inuit child riding the actual sled. The story of DAN McGREW is told through the jigsawed wooden pieces covered with lithographed paper. A flip book can put Nancy GREENE on skates or make her namesakes Graham and Lorne do a switch-about in television land. Even the mighty parliamentary towers of OTTAWA turn into building blocks for its young citizens.

The illustrations for *Eh? to Zed* are an exploration of our cultural roots, of the artforms which, together with our words, have helped build our country. With a host of new cultures now adding to its shape, we can only imagine the wonderful objects that will arise in the years ahead. We salute a Canada where dictionaries change and culture forever renews itself.

Text Copyright © 2000 Kevin Major
Illustration Copyright © 2000 Alan Daniel
Published in the United States in 2001

Northern Lights Books for Children are published by
Red Deer Press
Room 813, MacKimmie Library Tower
2500 University Drive NW
Calgary Alberta Canada T2N 1N4

Acknowledgments
Edited for the Press by Peter Carver
Design by Blair Kerrigan/Glyphics
Printed in Canada by Friesens for Red Deer Press

Financial support provided by the Alberta Foundation for the Arts, a beneficiary of the Lottery Fund of the Government of Alberta, and by the Canada Council, the Department of Canadian Heritage and the University of Calgary.

COMMITTED TO THE DEVELOPMENT OF CULTURE AND THE ARTS

Canadian Cataloguing in Publication Data
Major, Kevin, 1949-
Eh? to zed
(Northern lights books for children)
ISBN 0-88995-222-1
1. Canada — Juvenile literature. 2. English language — Alphabet — Juvenile literature.
I. Daniel, Alan, 1939– II. Title. III. Series.
FC58.M33 2000   j971   C00-910479-8
F1008.2.M28 2000

5 4 3

For my family of Canadians
–Kevin Major

For Lea
–Alan Daniel

Canadian Grant

Arctic, apple, aurora, Anik
Bonhomme, Bluenose, beaver, bannock

Canadarm, Cavendish, chinook, caribou
Dory, dinosaur, dulse, Dan McGrew

Evangeline, evergreen, eh?, Expo
Fleur-de-lis, fiddlehead, Fox, Fogo

Gould, Gretzky, Greene, grizzly bear
Habitant, Horseshoe, humpback, hare

Imax, insulin, Iqaluit, ice blind
Jay, Jasper, Juno, jack pine

Klondike, komatik, kittiwake, kayak
Loon, lacrosse, Lillooet, lumberjack

Maple, moose, McClung, Mountie
Neepawa, narwhal, nickel, Napanee

Ogopogo, Ottawa, oil, osprey
Peterson, potlatch, poutine, Percé

Quahog, quarter horse, quints, Qu'Appelle
Rockies, railway, rodeo, Riel

Shediac, sockeye, spud, St-Hubert
Tuktoyaktuk, toque, totem, tourtière

Ungava, umiak, uranium, ulu
Voyageur, Villeneuve, Viking, Van Doo

Wheat, walleye, Wawa, waxwing
Xenon, xylograph, X-country, X-ing

Yarmouth, Yoho, York, Yellowhead
Zamboni, zipper, zinc, zed